Simply Wonderful

Five Children's Sermons And
Activity Pages For Advent And Christmas

Julia E. Bland

CSS Publishing Company, Inc., Lima, Ohio

Dedicated to
Tim, Elizabeth, Julianna, Nick, Joel, Sam, Ruth, Rebekah,
Peter, Sarah, Miriam, Danna, Sabrina, Hannah, and Luke

The original purchaser may photocopy material in this publication for use as it was intended (i.e. worship material for worship use; educational material for classroom use; dramatic material for staging or production). No additional permission is required from the publisher for such copying by the original purchaser only. Inquiries should be addressed to: Permissions, CSS Publishing Company, Inc., P.O. Box 4503, Lima, Ohio 45802-4503.

Scripture quotations are from the *New Revised Standard Version of the Bible*, copyright 1989 by the Division of Christian Education of the National Council of the Churches of Christ in the USA. Used by permission.

ISBN: 0-7880-1520-6

Table Of Contents

Introduction

I have chosen to use the words "simple" and "simply" often in this series of Advent and Christmas sermons because these words describe very well what took place when Jesus was born — and what can take place now.

According to the dictionary, the word "simple" can mean plain, or of low rank. Something done "simply" can mean it is done in a simple or plain manner. Or "simply" can mean absolutely or altogether.

Mary, Joseph, and Jesus were simple, plain, and of low rank, and certainly the birth was of low rank. Mary, Joseph, and Jesus were also altogether, absolutely willing and obedient to do God's will. The coming of Jesus, God's son, into our world was simply, altogether, absolutely wonderful. And we respond with simple faith. Thanks be to God for his indescribable gift!

For the visual aid, a nativity set is needed. If possible have a place available where the children gather and add that day's piece, leaving it in place each week until all parts of the nativity are assembled.

These lessons are planned so that each child may take back to the pew an activity sheet. One side is a coloring page for young children. The other side has word puzzles and games for older children. The lessons are not limited to morning worship, however. They may be used any time there is opportunity for Christian education of children.

Suggestions From The Author

Study the sermon so that you can tell it in your own words, using your own personality and with the needs of your local children in mind.

The sermon as given is to get you started. Be open to the Holy Spirit as he guides you to add your own personal observations.

If you need notes, make them small and tuck them inside your Bible at the page where you will be reading the Scripture.

Open the Bible and read from it. Children need to know that what you say really is from the Scriptures.

Ask questions and allow time for the children to answer. This will get them thinking and involved, but children can say unexpected things, so be ready to guide them back to the subject.

Before the worship hour, clip the activity sheet, a pencil, and crayons to a clipboard to be ready to hand to each child when the children's time is over.

As you pray and prepare, claim the Lord's promise in Isaiah 55:11:

> *So shall my word be that goes out from my mouth;*
> *it shall not return to me empty,*
> *but it shall accomplish that which I purpose,*
> *and succeed in the thing for which I sent it.*

May God bless your efforts.

Julia Bland

Mary, Simply Willing

God likes to use simple, ordinary people to do His work.

Scripture: Luke 1:26-38; Deuteronomy 6:5; Leviticus 19:18

Visual Aid: The figure of Mary from a nativity set

Handouts: Activity sheets

Advance Preparations: Copy enough activity sheets for each child to have one and have them ready to hand out when the lesson is over.

The Sermon:

Are you ready to start thinking about Christmas? Why do we have Christmas? Is it a celebration of the time when our Lord Jesus was born? As the days go by in December we are going to think about the main people who were there when Jesus was born.

*Here is a figure from a nativity set. Can you tell me who it represents? Yes, Mary, the mother of Jesus. Let's talk about Mary. In Luke chapter one we learn that Mary was a young woman living in a town called Nazareth. She was engaged to Joseph. God had a special message for her. It was so important that He sent His angel, Gabriel, to Mary. Verse 30 says: "The angel said to her, 'Do not be afraid, Mary, for you have found favor with God.'" Then he told her she would have a baby boy whose name was to be Jesus. He was to have that name because it means Savior. This son of hers would be the very son of God.

Mary found favor with God. That means God was pleased with Mary. What would please God? Years before, God had told His people to love Him (Deuteronomy 6:5). He had told His people to love each other (Leviticus 19:18). Mary must have tried hard to do what God had asked. So God was pleased and chose her to be the mother to Jesus. Mary was a simple, ordinary young woman, not rich or famous, but God likes to use simple, ordinary people to do His work. Verse 35 says that God promised to give her power. That means He would help her. God doesn't ask anyone to serve Him without also helping them to do it. What did Mary say to the angel? Verse 38 says: "Then Mary said, 'Here am I, the servant of the Lord; let it be with me according to your word.'"

Mary was a simple, ordinary young woman, but she was special, too, because she was willing to do what God asked. She didn't make excuses. What if she had said any of the following? "I can't, we don't have any money saved." "This interferes with all my plans." "What if Joseph objects?" "The whole thing makes me nervous." Mary said none of this. "Here am I; let it be," she said. Mary was simply willing.

You and I will never be asked of God to do what Mary did. But God would like us to love and serve Him in other ways, without excuse. God wants us to be simply willing to do His will. We are simple, ordinary people, too, so what can we do? At home with Mom and Dad, sisters and brothers, we can be kind and loving, just as Mary was. We can be kind and loving with all others too. What else can you think of? *(Discuss)* Yes, we can share, pray, be in Sunday school, invite others, forgive, sing, and so on. We won't make excuses, will we? We can learn from Mary. God can use simple, ordinary people who are willing.

*Use visual aid

Joseph, Simply Believed And Obeyed

God depends on people who believe and obey.

Scripture: Matthew 1:18-21, 2:13-14

Visual Aid: The figure of Joseph from a nativity set

Handouts: Activity sheets

Advance Preparations: Copy enough activity sheets for each child to have one and have them ready to hand out when the lesson is over.

The Sermon:

The last time we were together we talked about *Mary. God chose Mary to be mother of His son Jesus and she was willing. Mary was a simple, ordinary person but God likes to use ordinary people to do His work.

*Here is another figure from the nativity set. Who do you think this one represents? Yes, Joseph. What kind of man do you think Joseph was? We know that he was engaged to Mary. He worked hard. Do you know the kind of work Joseph did? He was a carpenter. Joseph was a simple, ordinary person too, but he loved God and he loved others. We know that, because the Bible says he was a righteous man (v. 19). God chose Joseph to be the earthly father of His son Jesus.

But Joseph did wonder if he should get involved with Mary after all. He thought about this and as he did, God sent an angel with a message. The angel came in a dream, and in Matthew 1:20b and 21 we read that he said: "Joseph, son of David, do not be afraid to take Mary as your wife ... She will bear a son, and you are to name him Jesus, for he will save his people from their sins." Joseph obeyed the message God sent through His angel. Mary became his wife. Joseph simply believed and obeyed.

When we read more of this story in Matthew, we learn that after Jesus was born the wicked King Herod wanted to find the baby Jesus in order to kill him. An angel came to Joseph again and said: " 'Get up, take the child and his mother, and flee to Egypt, and remain there until I tell you; for Herod is about to search for the child, to destroy him.' Then Joseph got up, took the child and his mother by night, and went to Egypt ..." (Matthew 2:13b-14).

Joseph was a simple, ordinary man, but he was special too, because he believed and obeyed God. God depends on people who believe and obey Him.

Joseph got up from bed and right away he took Mary and Jesus and left for the country of Egypt. He didn't say any of the following: "Wouldn't next week do?" "This will ruin my carpentry business." "I can't believe that." "Can't we just hide out for a little while?" Joseph said none of the these. He immediately obeyed God. What might have happened if he had not believed and obeyed God? Would the baby have been killed? God depends on people who will believe and obey. Do we?

God will probably not send us angels with messages. He will not ask us to do as Joseph did. But He wants us to believe and obey. How do we know what to believe and obey? The Bible tells us. The Bible is a message from God. That is why it is so important to come to Sunday school and church and listen to Bible stories and hear the Bible taught and preached. We need to learn to read it ourselves. And when we know what God wants, how He wants us to live, we need to believe and obey.

What are some things God tells us and we should obey? *(Discuss)* Yes, we should obey our parents, be careful what we say or do that might hurt someone, treat others just as we want them to treat us, and so on.

We can learn from Joseph. God depends on ordinary people to simply believe and obey Him.

*Use visual aid

Jesus, Simply Human

Jesus can help because he, too, was human.

Scripture: 2 Corinthians 8:9; Philippians 2:6-8; Hebrews 2:17-18, 4:14-16

Visual Aid: The figure of baby Jesus from a nativity set

Handouts: Activity sheets

Advance Preparations: Copy enough activity sheets for each child to have one and have them ready to hand out when the lesson is over.

The Sermon:

We've talked about *Mary and *Joseph. Even though Mary and Joseph were simple, ordinary people God chose them to be the earthly parents of His son Jesus. Why did He choose them? They were willing and obedient to God. God had a plan.

God saw that most people were in trouble. They didn't know or love God. They didn't know how to live happy lives. They were unkind to one another. They were worried and afraid. So God had a plan. He would send His son Jesus into the world as a simple human being to show people how to live, to show everyone how much he loved them even if it meant he would die for them (Philippians 2:6-8).

*Who does this figure from the nativity set represent? Yes, Jesus. Jesus was to be an ordinary baby growing up in a simple home. In this way he would be just like we and most people are. Jesus was simply human. As a baby he had to learn to smile, sit up, crawl, walk, and talk.

As a boy he had to have lessons and do chores, maybe even babysit his younger brothers and sisters. When he was older he learned from Joseph how to be a carpenter, and he had to work in the carpenter's shop. He probably had to talk to disagreeable customers and folks who didn't want to pay their bills. He got hungry, thirsty, and tired. Besides this, we know that he also liked friends and parties. Yes, Jesus was simply human. Since Jesus was human and did all of these things, that means that he understands us.

When you have to go to school and learn lessons, when you have to help Mom and Dad, or when you are tired or hungry, remember that Jesus understands. Knowing that he understands how we feel helps us to talk to him in prayer about anything — good things or troubles (Hebrews 2:17-18, 4:14-16).

Jesus left a beautiful heavenly home to do this for us. 2 Corinthians 8:9 says: "For you know the generous act of our Lord Jesus Christ, that though he was rich, yet for your sakes he became poor...."

He, too, was willing and obedient to God's plan to help us, to give us a Savior, *this little baby, a human baby in a simple home.

*Use visual aid

God Is With Us, Simply Wonderful

If we are willing, believe, and obey, Jesus is with us.

Scripture: Luke 2:8-11; Matthew 1:23; John 14:15-16

Visual Aid: Figures of shepherds and angels from a nativity set

Handouts: Activity sheets

Advance Preparations: Copy enough activity sheets for each child to have one and have them ready to hand out when the lesson is over.

The Sermon:

We've been talking about Jesus and his family. Do you remember? *Mary was a simple, ordinary young woman, but she was willing to do what God asked. God likes to use simple, ordinary people to do His work. *Joseph was a simple, ordinary man but he believed God and obeyed Him. God depends on people who believe and obey.

*Jesus left his beautiful heavenly home to become a simple, ordinary baby growing up in a simple, ordinary home. He was obedient and wiling to do what God asked. Since Jesus was human, he understands and can help us. Because each of them was willing and obedient and believed God, something wonderful happened. Let's read in Luke 2:8-11: "In that region there were shepherds living in the fields, keeping watch over their flock by night. Then an angel of the Lord stood before them, and the glory of the Lord shone around them, and they were terrified. But the angel said to them, 'Do not be afraid; for see — I am bringing you good news of great joy for all the people: to you is born this day in the city of David a Savior, who is the Messiah, the Lord.'"

*Angels came from heaven the night Jesus was born. They came to *shepherds out in the fields taking care of sheep. The angels said Jesus was the Lord himself coming to live with people. Another name given to Jesus is Emmanuel. This name means "God is with us" (Matthew 1:23). God with us — that's simply wonderful!

God wanted to live with us, to be ordinary, to be poor as most people of the world are, so that He could show us how to be ordinary and yet happy. He wanted us to know how to be simple and yet love and please God. He wanted to show us how much He loved us all even if it meant He must die sometime to prove it.

Since then Jesus has gone back to heaven. Yet he still wants to live with us. How does he do that? He lives with us through his Holy Spirit. We must want him, love him, let him be our Savior, and be willing and obedient to do what he asks. Then his Holy Spirit lives with us wherever we are. He is with us at school, at the ball game, at parties, on vacation, when we sit down to eat, when we do chores, when we go to bed, when we watch television, and when we go to church. If we remember that Jesus is always with us, it will help us to be the good, kind, loving persons he wants us to be.

God is with us. That's simply wonderful!

*What did the shepherds do when the angels left them? Yes, they traveled into Bethlehem to see the wonderful baby who was the Lord himself coming to live with people.

*Use visual aid

Jesus — God's Gift — Simply Accept Him

Eternal life and the gift of Jesus as Savior is free, but we must take the gift.

Scripture: Romans 6:23b; Philippians 2:7b-8; 2 Corinthians 9:15

Visual Aid: A gift you received for Christmas; wise men from the nativity set

Handouts: Activity sheets

Advance Preparations: Copy enough activity sheets for each child to have one and have them ready to hand out when the lesson is over.

The Sermon:

Did you receive gifts for Christmas? Christmas is a time for giving and receiving, and we think it is fun, don't we? When Jesus was born, some who came to see him brought gifts. Do you know who they were? *Yes, the wise men.

*I received a gift. I really like it. What did you receive? Did you have to pay for your gifts? It wouldn't be a gift if you had to pay. A gift does not cost you anything. But gifts do cost someone something. Gifts cost money to buy them or time and work to make them. We give gifts to people we love. Gifts are to be accepted, taken, used, or enjoyed.

Did you stuff your gifts in the closet or under the bed, never to look or use or wear or play with them again? What would the person who gave you the gift think? Would it hurt their feelings?

At Christmas we celebrate Jesus, God's great gift to us. Romans 6:23b says: "The free gift of God is eternal life in Christ Jesus our Lord." The eternal life and gift of Jesus as Savior is free. It cost us nothing.

But, it cost God. Let's read Philippians 2:7b-8: "And being found in human form, he humbled himself and became obedient to the point of death — even death on a cross."

The gift of Jesus and eternal life cost him death on the cross. Do we say we love Jesus, yet act like we don't want him around? Kind of like stuffing a gift under the bed or in the closet? Or perhaps like leaving him out in the stable where he was born?

Just as other gifts are to be taken and used and enjoyed, God wants us to take Jesus as Lord and Savior and let him be a part of our lives. Jesus is God's gift to us. Simply accept him. Second Corinthians 9:15 says: "Thanks be to God for his indescribable gift!" Let us accept the gift of Jesus as our Lord and let us, too, give thanks for God's wonderful gift of a Savior and eternal life!

*Use visual aid

Mary was willing to do what God asked.

11

God likes to use simple, ordinary people to do his work.

The angel said to her, "Do not be afraid, Mary, for you have found favor with God."

Then Mary said, "Here am I, the servant of the Lord; let it be with me according to your word." Luke 1:38

Down then Across

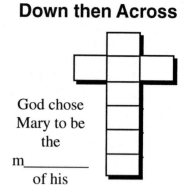

God chose Mary to be the

m_____

of his

s_____.

Find these words. They go down or to the right.

S	E	N	T	W	X	F	I	T	A	M
S	O	R	D	I	N	A	R	Y	N	X
I	T	M	K	L	O	V	E	D	G	P
M	H	A	I	L	M	O	T	H	E	R
P	E	R	N	I	A	R	E	E	L	A
L	R	Y	D	N	Z	B	E	L	X	Y
E	S	I	N	G	H	E	L	P	D	O
T	M	E	S	S	A	G	E	X	B	E

Mary
Simple
Ordinary
Loved
Help (2 times)
Others
Sent
Angel
Message
Favor

Am
Willing
Let
It
Be (2 times)
Mother
Are
Kind
Do
Pray
Sing

rich   do   pleased
loved   famous   town
ordinary   willing   favor
engaged   ordinary
mother   others

Fill in the blanks from the list of words.

Mary was an _ _ _ _ _ _ _ _ young woman.

She was not _ _ _ _ or _ _ _ _ _ _ _.

Mary was _ _ _ _ _ _ _ to Joseph.

She lived in a _ _ _ _ called Nazareth.

The Bible says Mary found _ _ _ _ _ with God.

God was _ _ _ _ _ _ _ with her.

Mary _ _ _ _ _ God and she loved _ _ _ _ _ _.

She was _ _ _ _ _ _ _ to do what God asked.

God likes to use simple, _ _ _ _ _ _ _ _ people to do his work.

Mary was the _ _ _ _ _ _ of Jesus, God's Son.

Are you willing to _ _ what God asks?

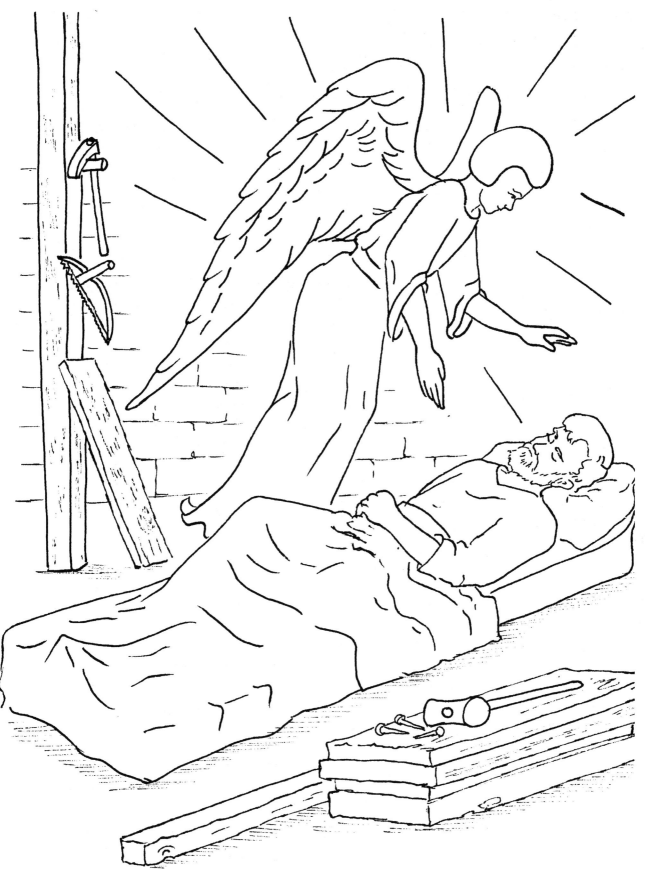

Joseph believed and obeyed God.

13

Down then Across

God chose __ __ __ __ __ __

to be the earthly

father of his __ __ __, Jesus.

… an angel said, "Joseph, son of David, do not be afraid to take Mary as your wife … she will bear a son, and you are to name him Jesus, for he will save his people from their sins."
Matthew 1:20b–21

God depends on people who will believe and obey.

Fill in the blanks using words from the list.

Joseph was a __ __ __ __ __ __ __ __ __ __. He was __ __ __ __ __ __ __ __ to Mary. He was a __ __ __ __ __ __ __, ordinary man, but God chose him to be the __ __ __ __ __ __ __ father of Jesus. An angel brought a __ __ __ __ __ __ __ __ to Joseph from God. Joseph was to take Mary for his __ __ __ __. Joseph __ __ __ __ __ __. After Jesus was born the __ __ __ __ __ came to Joseph with another message. Joseph was to get up and go to __ __ __ __ __. The wicked King Herod wanted to kill the __ __ __ __ Jesus. Joseph __ __ __ __ __ __ __ __ and __ __ __ __ __ __ God. God's message comes to us in the __ __ __ __ __. God depends on simple, ordinary people who will __ __ __ __ __ __ __ and __ __ __ __.

message	simple
angel	baby
carpenter	believed
obeyed	Bible
engaged	obey
wife	earthly
Egypt	obeyed
	believe

Find these words. They go down or to the right.

Joseph	Work	Angel	Son
Simple	Hard	Believed	Earth
Ordinary	Sent	Obeyed	Love
Carpenter	Real	The	Depends

Carpenters build houses. Here is part of a house. Which part below will finish it? Circle it.

C	O	B	E	Y	E	D	X
A	D	E	P	E	N	D	S
R	X	L	O	V	E	X	J
P	S	I	M	P	L	E	O
E	O	E	A	R	T	H	S
N	N	V	N	S	W	H	E
T	H	E	G	E	O	A	P
E	X	D	E	N	R	R	H
R	E	A	L	T	K	D	X
O	R	D	I	N	A	R	Y

14

Jesus left his home in heaven to become like we are so that he could help us.

Down then Across

Jesus u __ __ __ __ __ __ __ __ __ __ __ __ us

because he was human and lived on e __ __ __ __

in a simple home, like most of us do.

Jesus can help because he, too, was human.

For you know the generous act of our Lord Jesus Christ, that though he was rich, yet for your sakes he became poor…

2 Corinthians 8:9

Find the words that are in the list. They go down or to the right.

Understands
Us
He
Human
We
Grew
Learn
Walk
Smile
Boy

Work
Joseph
Hungry
Thirsty
Tired
Simple
Home
Friends
Parties
Die
Pray

J	H	T	H	I	R	S	T	Y	B	O	Y
O	U	N	D	E	R	S	T	A	N	D	S
S	N	U	S	H	W	E	I	X	H	G	W
E	G	H	E	U	W	O	R	K	O	R	A
P	R	S	I	M	P	L	E	X	M	E	L
H	Y	P	R	A	Y	X	D	I	E	W	K
F	R	I	E	N	D	S	L	E	A	R	N
S	M	I	L	E	P	A	R	T	I	E	S

Use words from the list to fill in the blanks.

Jesus left his __ __ __ __ in heaven to be born a __ __ __ __ __

in an __ __ __ __ __ __ __ __ home. He had to grow and

__ __ __ __ __ just as we do. He had to learn to __ __ __ __

and talk, do __ __ __ __ __ __ __ and work __ __ __ __.

He became a __ __ __ __ __ __ __ __ __ like Joseph. He got

__ __ __ __ __ __ and __ __ __ __ __ __ __ and __ __ __ __.

Jesus liked __ __ __ __ __ __ __ and parties. He can help us

because he was __ __ __ __ __ like we are and

__ __ __ __ __ __ __ __ __ __ __. We can __ __ __ __ knowing that he will help.

pray
human
home
baby
tired
thirsty
ordinary
learn

hungry
carpenter
hard
lessons
walk
friends
understands

16

Jesus is God with us.

17

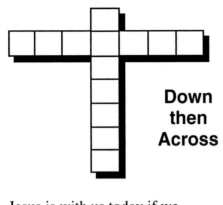

Down then Across

Jesus is with us today if we

are w__ __ __ __ __ __, if we

b__ __ __ __ __ __ and obey him.

To you is born this day in the city of David a Savior, who is the Messiah, the Lord. Luke 2:11

If we are willing, believe and obey, Jesus is with us.

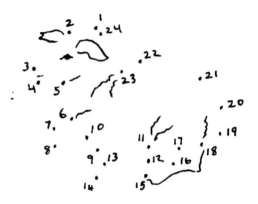

Find the words that are in the list. They go down or to the right.

B	O	W	I	L	L	I	N	G	W	J
A	B	O	R	N	L	I	V	E	O	O
B	E	W	I	T	H	O	M	E	N	Y
Y	D	L	O	V	E	U	L	H	D	F
X	I	D	I	E	A	S	O	U	E	O
B	E	L	I	E	V	E	V	M	R	R
A	N	G	E	L	E	W	E	A	F	A
S	T	I	L	L	N	E	D	N	U	L
S	H	E	P	H	E	R	D	S	L	L

Willing   Die
Obedient   Angel
Home   Shepherds
Heaven   Believe
Born   Love
Baby   Still
Live   We
With   Joy
Us   For
Human   All
Loved   Wonderful

Use words from the list to fill in the blanks.

Angels came from heaven the night Jesus was born. They came to

__ __ __ __ __ __ __ __ __ who were out taking care of their __ __ __ __ __.

An __ __ __ __ __ __ said that there was news of great __ __ __ for all people.

A savior, the Lord himself, had come to __ __ __ __ as we do in our ordinary,

__ __ __ __ __ __ home. He was coming to show us how much God __ __ __ __ __

us, even if that meant he would someday __ __ __ for us. Jesus has gone back to

__ __ __ __ __ __ but he is __ __ __ __ __ with all who __ __ __ __ __ __ __ __ ,

love, and __ __ __ __ him. His Holy Spirit is with us and __ __ __ __ __ us wherever

we are, at school, at home, at church, on vacation, at parties. God is with us.

Simply wonderful!

angel
loves
die
heaven
believe
shepherds
live
joy
sheep
simple
helps
still
obey

18

Jesus is God's gift to us.

Two go down then one across.

The f__ __ __ g__ __ __ of Jesus
and e__ __ __ __ __ __ life cost him
his death on the cross. Let's accept
this gift from God — Jesus as Savior!

Eternal life and the gift
of Jesus as Savior is
free, but we must
take the gift.

The free gift of God is
eternal life in
Christ Jesus our Lord.
Romans 6:23b

Find the words that are in the list. They go down or to the right.

D	F	R	E	E	G	U	S	S	A
E	R	E	C	E	I	V	E	A	C
A	B	A	B	Y	F	U	N	V	C
T	O	C	O	S	T	M	T	I	E
H	R	X	W	I	S	E	A	O	P
O	N	L	I	F	E	N	K	R	T
C	R	O	S	S	O	B	E	Y	X
E	T	E	R	N	A	L	O	V	E

Receive	On
Gifts	Cross
Fun	Life
Wise	Eternal
Men	Savior
Baby	Take
Born	Accept
Cost	Love
Free	Obey
Death	Us

Fill in the blanks with words from the list.

cost   gifts
use   baby
free   receive
life   someone
death
work
Christmas
indescribable

Wise men brought __ __ __ __ __ to the __ __ __ __ Jesus. We like to give
and __ __ __ __ __ __ __ gifts, especially at __ __ __ __ __ __ __ __ __ __.
We __ __ __ the gifts we receive. A gift does not __ __ __ __ us, but it does
cost __ __ __ __ __ __ __ money, time or __ __ __ __. God gave us a gift.
The __ __ __ __ gift of God is eternal __ __ __ __ in Jesus Christ our Lord.
This gift cost Jesus__ __ __ __ __ on a cross. The Bible says, "Thanks be to God
for his __ __ __ __ __ __ __ __ __ __ __ __ gift!" (2 Corinthians 9:15)

20

ANSWER KEYS
for
ACTIVITY PAGES

God likes to use simple, ordinary people to do his work.

The angel said to her, "Do not be afraid, Mary, for you have found favor with God."

Then Mary said, "Here am I, the servant of the Lord; let it be with me according to your word." Luke 1:38

Down then Across

God chose Mary to be the m̲o̲t̲h̲e̲r̲ of his s̲o̲n̲.

Find these words. They go down or to the right.

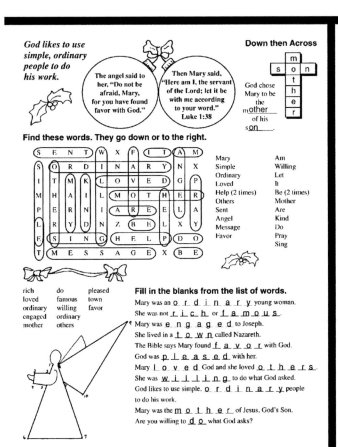

Mary
Simple
Ordinary
Loved
Help (2 times)
Others
Sent
Angel
Message
Favor

Am
Willing
Let
It
Be (2 times)
Mother
Are
Kind
Do
Pray
Sing

rich   do   pleased
loved   famous   town
ordinary   willing   favor
engaged   ordinary
mother   others

Fill in the blanks from the list of words.

Mary was an o̲r̲d̲i̲n̲a̲r̲y̲ young woman.
She was not r̲i̲c̲h̲ or f̲a̲m̲o̲u̲s̲.
Mary was e̲n̲g̲a̲g̲e̲d̲ to Joseph.
She lived in a t̲o̲w̲n̲ called Nazareth.
The Bible says Mary found f̲a̲v̲o̲r̲ with God.
God was p̲l̲e̲a̲s̲e̲d̲ with her.
Mary l̲o̲v̲e̲d̲ God and she loved o̲t̲h̲e̲r̲s̲.
She was w̲i̲l̲l̲i̲n̲g̲ to do what God asked.
God likes to use simple, o̲r̲d̲i̲n̲a̲r̲y̲ people to do his work.
Mary was the m̲o̲t̲h̲e̲r̲ of Jesus, God's Son.
Are you willing to d̲o̲ what God asks?

Down then Across

God chose J̲o̲s̲e̲p̲h̲ to be the earthly father of his s̲o̲n̲, Jesus.

... an angel said, "Joseph, son of David, do not be afraid to take Mary as your wife ... she will bear a son, and you are to name him Jesus, for he will save his people from their sins." Matthew 1:20b–21

God depends on people who will believe and obey.

Fill in the blanks using words from the list.

Joseph was a c̲a̲r̲p̲e̲n̲t̲e̲r̲. He was e̲n̲g̲a̲g̲e̲d̲ to Mary. He was a s̲i̲m̲p̲l̲e̲, ordinary man, but God chose him to be the e̲a̲r̲t̲h̲l̲y̲ father of Jesus. An angel brought a m̲e̲s̲s̲a̲g̲e̲ to Joseph from God. Joseph was to take Mary for his w̲i̲f̲e̲. Joseph o̲b̲e̲y̲e̲d̲. After Jesus was born the a̲n̲g̲e̲l̲ came to Joseph with another message. Joseph was to get up and go to E̲g̲y̲p̲t̲. The wicked King Herod wanted to kill the b̲a̲b̲y̲ Jesus. Joseph b̲e̲l̲i̲e̲v̲e̲d̲ and o̲b̲e̲y̲e̲d̲ God. God's message comes to us in the B̲i̲b̲l̲e̲. God depends on simple, ordinary people who will b̲e̲l̲i̲e̲v̲e̲ and o̲b̲e̲y̲.

message   simple
angel   baby
carpenter believed
obeyed   Bible
engaged   obey
wife   earthly
Egypt   obeyed
           believe

Find these words. They go down or to the right.

Joseph   Work   Angel   Son
Simple   Hard   Believed   Earth
Ordinary   Sent   Obeyed   Love
Carpenter Real   The   Depends

Carpenters build houses. Here is part of a house. Which part below will finish it? Circle it.

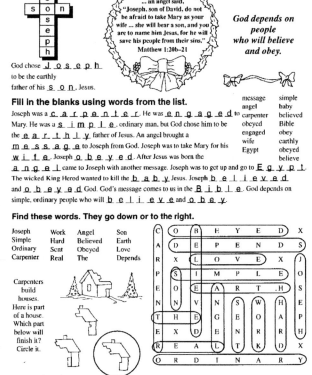

Down then Across

Jesus u n d e r s t a n d s us because he was human and lived on e a r t h in a simple home, like most of us do.

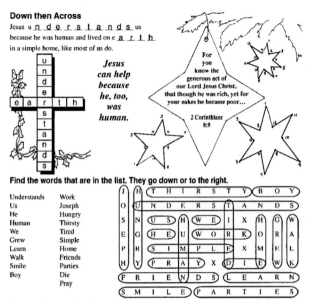

Jesus can help because he, too, was human.

For you know the generous act of our Lord Jesus Christ, that though he was rich, yet for your sakes he became poor...

2 Corinthians 8:9

Find the words that are in the list. They go down or to the right.

Understands	Work
Us	Joseph
He	Hungry
Human	Thirsty
We	Tired
Grew	Simple
Learn	Home
Walk	Friends
Smile	Parties
Boy	Die
	Pray

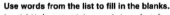

Use words from the list to fill in the blanks.

Jesus left his h o m e in heaven to be born a b a b y in an o r d i n a r y home. He had to grow and l e a r n just as we do. He had to learn to w a l k and talk, do l e s s o n s and work h a r d. He became a c a r p e n t e r like Joseph. He got h u n g r y and t h i r s t y and t i r e d. Jesus liked f r i e n d s and parties. He can help us because he was h u m a n like we are and u n d e r s t a n d s. We can p r a y knowing that he will help.

pray	hungry
human	carpenter
home	hard
baby	lessons
tired	walk
thirsty	friends
ordinary	understands
learn	

Down then Across

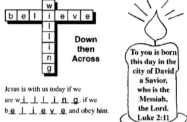

Jesus is with us today if we are w i l l i n g, if we b e l i e v e and obey him.

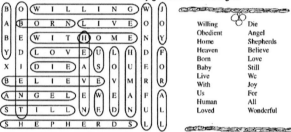

To you is born this day in the city of David a Savior, who is the Messiah, the Lord. Luke 2:11

If we are willing, believe and obey, Jesus is with us.

Find the words that are in the list. They go down or to the right.

Willing	Die
Obedient	Angel
Home	Shepherds
Heaven	Believe
Born	Love
Baby	Still
Live	We
With	Joy
Us	For
Human	All
Loved	Wonderful

Use words from the list to fill in the blanks.

Angels came from heaven the night Jesus was born. They came to s h e p h e r d s who were out taking care of their s h e e p. An a n g e l said that there was news of great j o y for all people. A savior, the Lord himself, had come to l i v e as we do in our ordinary, s i m p l e home. He was coming to show us how much God l o v e s us, even if that meant he would someday d i e for us. Jesus has gone back to h e a v e n but he is s t i l l with all who b e l i e v e, love, and o b e y him. His Holy Spirit is with us and h e l p s us wherever we are, at school, at home, at church, on vacation, at parties. God is with us. Simply wonderful!

angel
loves
die
heaven
believe
shepherds
live
joy
sheep
simple
helps
still
obey

Two go down then one across.

The f r e e g i f t of Jesus and e t e r n a l life cost him his death on the cross. Let's accept this gift from God — Jesus as Savior!

Eternal life and the gift of Jesus as Savior is free, but we must take the gift.

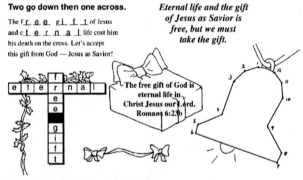

The free gift of God is eternal life in Christ Jesus our Lord. Romans 6:23

Find the words that are in the list. They go down or to the right.

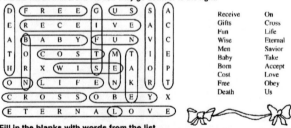

Receive	On
Gifts	Cross
Fun	Life
Wise	Eternal
Men	Savior
Baby	Take
Born	Accept
Cost	Love
Free	Obey
Death	Us

Fill in the blanks with words from the list.

cost	gifts
use	baby
free	receive
life	someone
death	
work	
Christmas	
indescribable	

Wise men brought g i f t s to the b a b y Jesus. We like to give and r e c e i v e gifts, especially at C h r i s t m a s. We u s e the gifts we receive. A gift does not c o s t us, but it does cost s o m e o n e money, time or w o r k. God gave us a gift. The f r e e gift of God is eternal l i f e in Jesus Christ our Lord. This gift cost Jesus d e a t h on a cross. The Bible says, "Thanks be to God for his i n d e s c r i b a b l e gift!" (2 Corinthians 9:15)